MODAL MAS[TERY]

for
Guitar Improvisation

by
MIKE PACHELLI

JOE GOLDFEDER MUSIC ENTERPRISES, INC.
P.O. BOX 660, LYNBROOK, N.Y. 11563

About The Author

Experience is the best teacher! The next best thing is a teacher with experience. Mike Pachelli is a teacher with experience that has led him through a maze of night clubs, concert halls and recording studios for the past 15 years.

Jazz critic Leonard Feather says, "Mike Pachelli . . . has a loose, extrovert style with chops to spare, and a mature blues feeling." That "loose, extrovert style" and "blues feeling" comes from confidence gained by hard work. Mike has toured with organist Jack McDuff, studied with Joe Pass and "gigged" with Larry Elgart and Ferrante and Teicher among others.

One of the signs of maturity in a musician is to have no fear of sharing things learned over the years. Pachelli is now ready to share some of the technique that made L.A. Examiner jazz critic David Weiss say, "Pachelli's driving improvisations are alone worth the price of admission." I say anything that provides insight into the always tasteful, sometimes breathtaking solos that flow from Pachelli's guitar is priceless. Blues great Albert King was so taken with Mike's playing he offered him a touring position having heard just a few tunes.

Read, study and enjoy **MODAL MASTERY FOR GUITAR IMPROVISATION.**

DAVID GRAY host of **JAZZ MILESTONES ON WBBW RADIO.**

INDEX

PREFACE

This book was written while I was on the road with Jack McDuff who was gracious enough to let me experiment with these principals on the band stand.

I would like to thank Joe Pass, Phil Keaggy, and Pat Martino for their guidance, instruction, and friendship in helping me to see the possibilities of our brother instrument.

Special thanks to Gerry Teifer at ATV Music Group for all his help.

Introduction

The purpose of this book shall be to give the guitarist an understanding of the Diatonic Modes. It came, to the authors' attention after much searching and talking with both students and colleagues that there was virtually no written material on modal improvisation for guitar.

The Diatonic (also called 'Church') Modes were named after Greek tribes because when these scales were first constructed it was believed that they were the same as the scales used in ancient Greek music. This turned out to be incorrect so it is not necessary to learn the Greek scale forms as there isn't any music based upon them that has survived.

Diatonic modal knowledge is essential to the guitarist as a tool to be used for soloing. A solo should be a spontaneous improvisation. **MODAL MASTERY** can help store enough information to free yourself from having to search for what you want to play, thus aiding in spontaneity.

Modes can best be understood by thinking of them as 'moods'. Each of the seven Diatonic Modes has a particular mood it best describes, however, by inter-relating these 'moods' against a particular chord or series of chords the improviser can obtain many interesting harmonic possibilities. This is not the only knowledge necessary to become a great improviser but **MODAL MASTERY** can be essential in giving you a clear picture of modal usage.

To be a tasteful improviser we must have a large musical vocabulary and be a technical master of our instrument. **MODAL MASTERY** can help you achieve that goal. In conclusion, to quote Charlie Parker, "First, master your instrument. Then, forget all that . . . and play."

IONIAN MODE

The Ionian mode is probably the most famous of all, having been popularized in every grammar school with the Do-Re-Mi- song. I will start with this mode because it is our Major Scale. Since I will be relating this book to the guitar, I'll start with "G" because it falls on the neck in such a way as to give the clearest picture.

This is the "G" Ionian Mode.

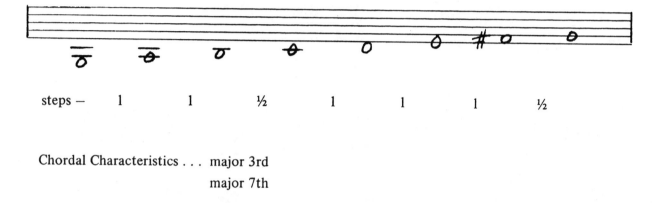

steps —   1   1   ½   1   1   1   ½

Chordal Characteristics . . . major 3rd
                        major 7th

The Ionian Mode can be constructed by equating seven tones — starting with a note then up a whole step, whole step, half step, whole step, whole step, whole step, half step. It can also be thought of as eight tones in whole steps except for a ½ step between the 3rd & 4th tone and a ½ step between the 7th & 8th tone.

solo usage — (against these chord types)   G natural
G major 7th
G 6
G 6/9
G sus
any G major sounding chord

Here is the fingering on the guitar for two octaves.

finger

1
2
3
4

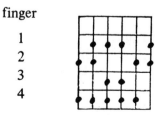

It is **imperative** that you master this fingering — it will give more flexibility & greater strength.

6

Suggested exercises to be done in all keys.

etc.

etc.

etc.

etc.

These exercises are intended to help technically master this mode. Soloing should not be simply scaler. You should make up your own exercises and find melodic paths of your own. Also experiment with different rhythms and rests. And most important of all — LISTEN!!!!

PRACTICE SUGGESTIONS

While playing this mode listen to its' "Major" gender.

Use a metronome at all times when practicing.

Do all exercises at different speeds. (This is essential to developing good time).

CHORD RELATIONS

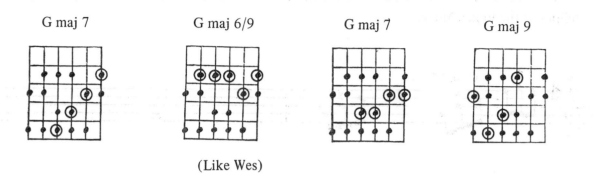

G maj 7   G maj 6/9   G maj 7   G maj 9

(Like Wes)

Use these relationships for arpeggio practice on this mode.
Practice these relationships in all keys!

The Ionian Mode has a finality about it. Its' sound is firm and definite as an introduction and an ending.

As you progress thru this book you will learn how it is possible to use the Ionian Mode (over any type of chord) when improvising. This is how the jazz musician achieves a polytonal effect when soloing. In other words, it is possible to interject one mood against another. Just as it is possible to have mixed emotions about a certain subject, so also can we mix our musical feelings thru **MODAL MASTERY**.

Here are some popular melodies based on the IONIAN MODE.

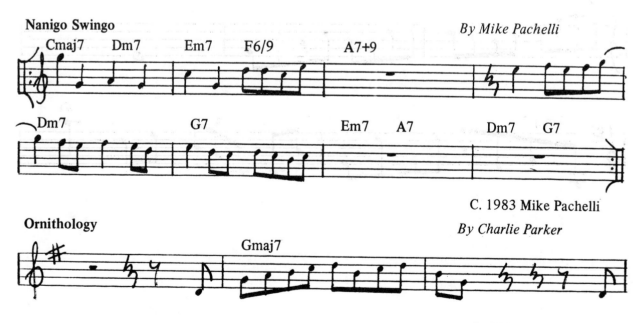

Nanigo Swingo   *By Mike Pachelli*

C. 1983 Mike Pachelli

Ornithology   *By Charlie Parker*

C. 1946 Atlantic Music Corp.
Used By Permission

Here are some phrases and (or) cliches that are based on the Ionian Mode. These are not given with the intention for the student to memorize but as an aid in hearing the harmonic possibilities of the Ionian Mode.

DORIAN MODE

The Dorian Mode is a minor (sounding) mode widely used in today's music. It is used widely in the church and also in jazz and rock tunes. It has a sad sound and a feel of motion. We will start with the "A" Dorian scale because it is like playing the "G" Ionian mode starting from the second scale degree (e.g.A) and keeping the Ionian scaler movement. Therefore "A" Dorian can be used as a first substitute for "G" Ionian.

This is the "A" Dorian Mode.

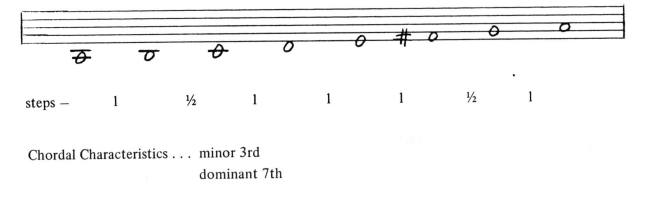

steps —   1   ½   1   1   1   ½   1

Chordal Characteristics . . . minor 3rd
dominant 7th

Here is the relationship between "G" Ionian and "A" Dorian.

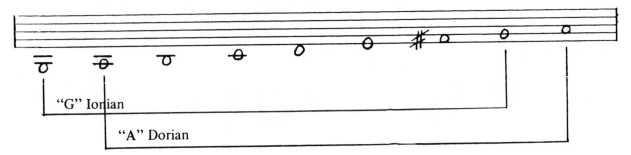

The Dorian Mode is constructed by starting on a note, going up a whole step, half step, whole step, whole step, whole step, half step, whole step, or it can be thought of as having ½ steps between the 2nd & 3rd and the 6th & 7th scale degrees, and whole steps between the rest of the scale degrees.

solo usage — (against these chord types)   A minor
A minor 7
A minor 9
A minor 6
A minor 11
any A minor sounding chord

Secondary usage . . . . .all G major type chords

Here is the guitar fingering for two octaves.

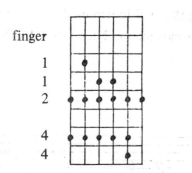

finger

1
1
2

4
4

I recommend this fingering and you will notice that the first finger works the 3rd and 4th fret and that the fourth finger works the 7th and 8th fret. For alternate fingering shift to first finger on the "E" note 5th fret of the "B" string.

Suggested exercises to be done in all keys.

PRACTICE SUGGESTIONS

While playing this mode listen to its' "Minor" gender.

Use a metronome at different speeds.

Practice the Dorian mode in all keys.

Play the "A" Dorian mode against "G" major type chords — Let your ear be the final judge.

CHORD RELATIONS

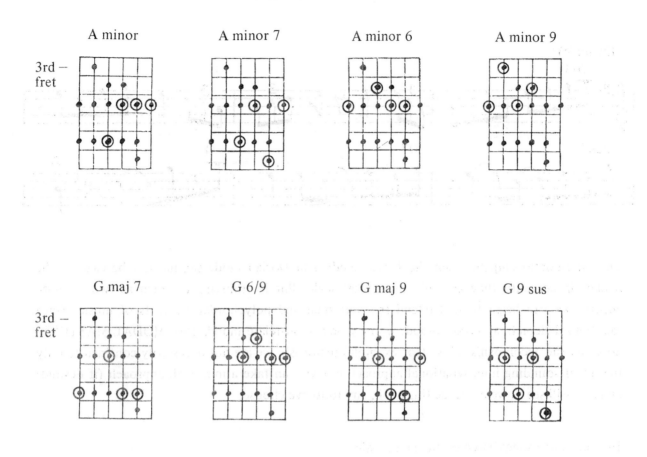

The Dorian mode works well in a II-V-I situation (e.g. Am7 to D7 to G)
Use the "A" Dorian mode against the Am7 and the D7, then switch to the "G" Ionian for the G chord.

(Example)

You can also stay on the "A" Dorian pattern thru out the changes and let your ear be the judge for some interesting polytonal and polychordal relationships.

(Example)

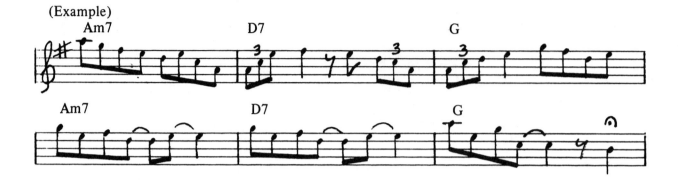

The inter-relationship between the Ionian mode and Dorian mode should now be clear to the reader. In actuality they are one (nine note) scale. But by thinking of them as two separate entities we can begin to understand the polytonal and polychordal elements of music. Since each chord depicts a certain mood, we may now inter-relate moods thru MODAL MASTERY. So when the accompanist plays (for example) major-ish, we are not necessarily confined to only the major sounding improvisational approach but we can take a minor-ish approach (if desired) or as we will see as we continue this book, any route we choose.

Here are some songs based on the Dorian Mode.

Sunday Stroll   *By Mike Pachelli*

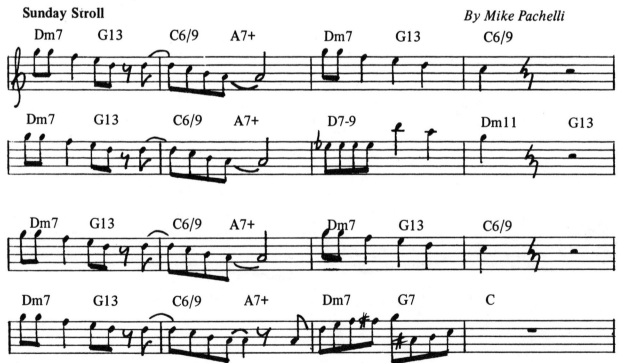

c. 1983 Mike Pachelli

Deputy Dawg

By Jack McDuff

To complete this chapter on the Dorian Mode, here are some phrases based upon it. Listen to the minor-ish sound of these phrases and experiment with your own licks. The Dorian Mode has an "outside" sounding harmonic possibility due to the major sixth interval against the minor third as in example four.*

PHRYGIAN MODE

The Phrygian Mode is a minor sounding mode and the first one in our diatonic series that contains some chord alterations (e.g. b9 +5) therefore it works well with these types of minor chords. The "B" Phrygian mode can be thought of as the second scalar extension of the "A" Dorian Mode and the third extension of the "G" Ionian Mode.

This is the "B" Phrygian Mode.

steps — ½   1   1   1   ½   1   1

Chordal Characteristics . . . minor 3rd
dominant 7th
flatted 9th
raised 5th
raised 11th

Here is the relationship between "G" Ionian, "A" Dorian, and "B" Phrygian.

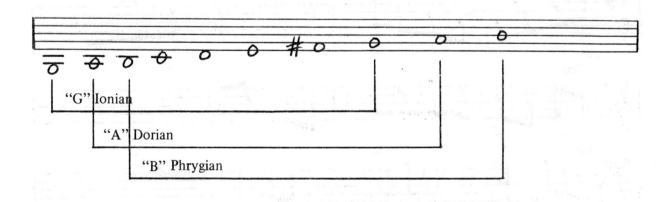

The Phrygian Mode is constructed in this series — ½ step, whole, whole, whole, ½, whole, whole. It can be thought of as a succession of whole tones except for in between the 1st & 2nd and 5th & 6th scale degrees which are half steps apart.

solo usage — (against these chord types)

B minor	B minor +5
B minor 7	any B minor sounding chord
B minor b9	
B minor II	
B minor + II	

secondary usage. . . . . .all A minor type chords

third usage. . . . . .all G major type chords

fourth usage . . . . .all E minor type chords

(this B Phrygian fingering contains a good E Minor scale fingering)

Here is the guitar fingering for two octaves of B Phrygian Mode

E Aeolian Mode

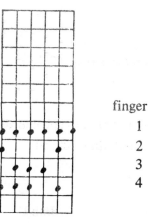

finger
1
2
3
4

Suggested exercises to be done in all keys.

PRACTICE SUGGESTIONS

Pay attention to the Phrygian's minor sound and it's chordal alterations (e.g. +5, b9).

Use the metronome at different speeds.

Practice the Phrygian Mode in all keys.

Play the "B" Phrygian Mode against "A" Minor type chords and "G" Major type chords.

Use the Phrygian Mode to give a slight altered effect against a natural Minor chord.

CHORD RELATIONS

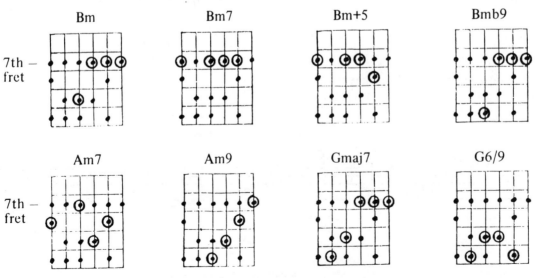

The "B" Phrygian Mode works well in a situation where "B" minor is moving to "E" minor since the "E" Dorian Mode is contained in this fingering. Use the "B" Phrygian Mode as the second extension of the "A" Dorian Mode. Playing in "B" Phrygian against "A" Dorian gives an "E" minor to "A" minor effect used in many rock and jazz fusion tunes.

Use "B" Phrygian as third extension of the "G" Ionian Mode. This gives a major seventh effect ala George Benson.

Here is an example of the "B" Phrygian usage in the style of George Benson.

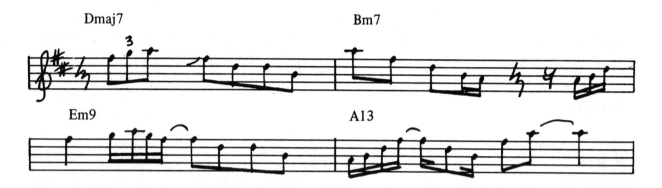

The Phrygian Mode has a Spanish flavor when used against a major chord. (e.g. "B" Phrygian against "B" Natural) This is the basis of many Spanish songs and Spanish sounding cliches.

The Phrygian Mode is also an excellent scale for fast Spanish sounding licks.
Again using its' Minor Third against a chord with a Major Third.

By playing out of "B" Phrygian over an "Am" we emphasize the ninth sound of an Am chord. Try resolving some lines to the tonic "B", (of "B" Phrygian) while someone plays an "Am7".

Example

By establishing the "Am" sound in the first few beats of the above example we sometimes feel obliged to start an improvisation on a direct chord tone, (root, third, fifth). By inter-relating "B" Phrygian and resolving our lines to its' tonic, we can easily break this habit.

If we play the same example against a "G" major seventh we emphasize the third scale degree of "G".

In actuality we are considering a ten note "G" major scale. But by thinking in terms of different modes we can learn every possible position to play out of "G" major, then by inter-relating modes we can master improvising over any chord in any position.

It should now be clear how **MODAL MASTERY** can file the information into your subconscious to free you from having to "search" while soloing.

Be sure to try the reverse of these examples by playing "G" Ionian against "Bm" type chords and "A" Dorian against "Bm" type chords.

LYDIAN MODE

The Lydian Mode is a major type mode almost exactly like the Ionian Mode except that the Ionians' perfect fourth is replaced with a flatted fifth in the Lydian Mode. The Lydian Mode is very popular in jazz improvisation because of its' flatted fifth against a major seventh sound. Use the Lydian Mode instead of the Ionian Mode when there is freedom to harmonically stretch out over a major sounding chord. The Lydian Mode can clash with a major chord so let your ear be the judge.

This is the "C" Lydian Mode

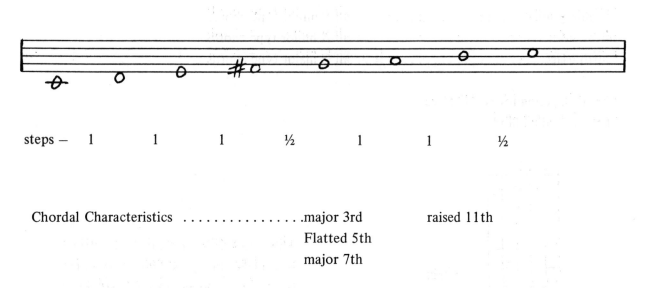

steps —   1   1   1   ½   1   1   ½

Chordal Characteristics . . . . .major 3rd   raised 11th
                                        Flatted 5th
                                        major 7th

Here is the relationship between "G" Ionian, "A" Dorian, "B" Phrygian and "C" Lydian.

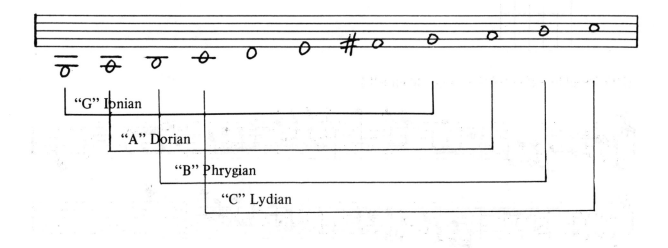

The sequential series of the Lydian Mode are as follows: whole step, whole step, whole step, half step, whole step, whole step, half step. It can be thought of as a succession of whole tones except for between the 4th & 5th scale degrees and the 7th & 8th degrees which have half steps.

solo usage — (against these chord types)   C

C major 7th

C major 7th flat 5

C raised 11th

any C major sounding chord for an

altered effect

secondary usage. . . . . .all B minor type chords

third usage. . . . . .all A minor type chords

fourth usage . . . . .all G major type chords

Here is fingering for two octaves
of the C Lydian Mode

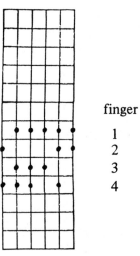

finger

1

2

3

4

This fingering contains a strong secondary minor sound — (e .g. for C — Em). When playing off of a raised eleventh chord. The two tonal centers are interchangeable.

Here are some exercises to be done in all keys.

21

etc.

etc.

etc.

etc.

PRACTICE SUGGESTIONS

Practice the Lydian Mode in all keys.

Use a metronome.

Play "C" Lydian against "B" Minor type chords, "A" Minor type chords, and "G" Major type chords.

Substitute the Lydian Mode where you have been using the Ionian mode, (for an altered effect).

CHORD RELATIONS

C maj 7th   C maj b5   C 6/9 b5   C maj 9 +11

8th —
fret

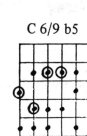
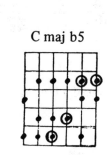

Bm7   Bm7 +5   Am7   Am11

8th —
fret

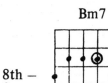

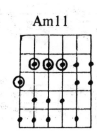

22

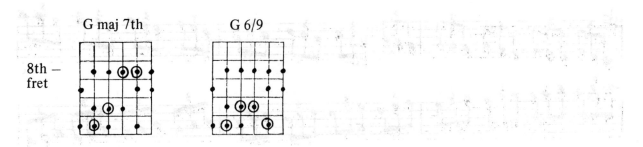

G maj 7th   G 6/9

8th —
fret

"C" Lydian works well when a "C" chord is moving to "E" minor, (the secondary minor of "C") since the "E" Natural Minor scale is easily accessable in this fingering.

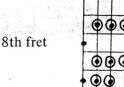

8th fret   "E" Natural Minor

Here is an excellent fast passage moving to "G" Major by playing the "C" Lydian Mode downward to the low "G" on the "E" strings for a "C" Major to "G" Major effect.

The Lydian Mode lends itself towards some beautiful raised 11th lines.

C 6/9 +11

C maj 7 +11

By playing in "C" Lydian against "G" Major type chords we create a suspension effect if we resolve our lines to the Lydian Tonic.

By using "C" Lydian against "A" Minor type chords we re-enforce the minor third of Am and can easily accentuate the 6th or 9th extension of Am via the Lydian's major seventh and flatted fifth.

Thinking of "C" Lydian as our tonic scale against a "Bm" chord creates a harmonically "outside" effect because it forces "Bm" into a raised fifth, flatted ninth situation.

Be sure to try the reverse of these examples, like playing in "G" Ionian against a "C" Major type chord; or "A" Dorian against a "C" Major type chord and "B" Phyrgian against "C" Major type chords.

24

Here is an excellent example of a tune based entirely on the Bb Lydian Mode. It can be used to improvise over the entire song.

Nemesis

By Mike Pachelli

MIXOLYDIAN MODE

The Mixolydian Mode is a dominant seventh type mode and probably the most important scale in jazz improvisation because of its' affinity with the blues. This mode in conjunction with the Blues Scale, (see page 31), can give the soloist a good foundation for improvisation on a twelve bar blues format. The Mixolydian Mode can be heard in every great jazz player and should be mastered for that "bluesy" sound in your playing.

This is the "D" Mixolydian Mode

steps —   1   1   ½   1   1   ½   1

The above sequential series should be inter-played with chromaticism in order to utilize the Mixolydians' full potential. For example play D — Eb(b9) — E and G — Ab(b5) — A. Also F natural can be used for the minor third against a major third "blues" effect.

Chordal Characteristics . . . . .Major 3rd
                                                       Dominant 7th

The Mixolydian Mode is a sequence of whole steps except for between the 3rd & 4th and the 6th & 7th scale degrees which are half steps.

solo usage — (against these chord types)   D7
                                             D9
                                             D13
                                             (all Dominant 7th type chords)
secondary usage. . . . . .all C major type chords
third usage. . . . . .all B minor type chords
fourth usage . . . . .all A minor type chords
fifth usage . . . . .all G major type chords
sixth usage. . . . . .the Blues in "D" (in conjunction
                                                         with the Blues Scale)

Here is the relationship between "G" Ionian, "A" Dorian, "B" Phrygian, "C" Lydian, and "D" Mixolydian.

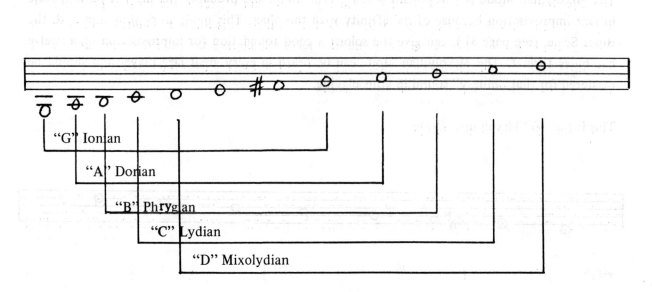

"G" Ionian

"A" Dorian

"B" Phrygian

"C" Lydian

"D" Mixolydian

The above example can be thought of as a 12 note "G" Ionian scale. Then inter-relate the corresponding modes for different polychordal effects.

Here is the Mixolydian Mode Guitar fingering for two octaves.

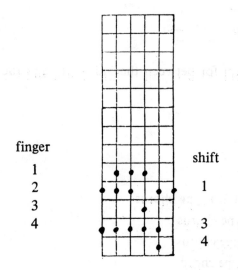

finger
1
2
3
4

shift
1

3
4

A shift is necessary with the first finger when reaching the "A" note (on the "B" string.)

Suggested exercises to be done in all keys.

etc.

etc.

PRACTICE SUGGESTIONS

Play the Mixolydian Mode in all keys using various rhythmns.

Use a metronome on the "UP" Beat to master a jazz feel for this Mode.

Play the Mixolydian Mode against a Blues Progression. (Let your ear be the judge.)

Play "D" Mixolydian against "C" Major, "B" Minor, "A" Minor, & "G" Major chord types.

CHORD RELATIONS

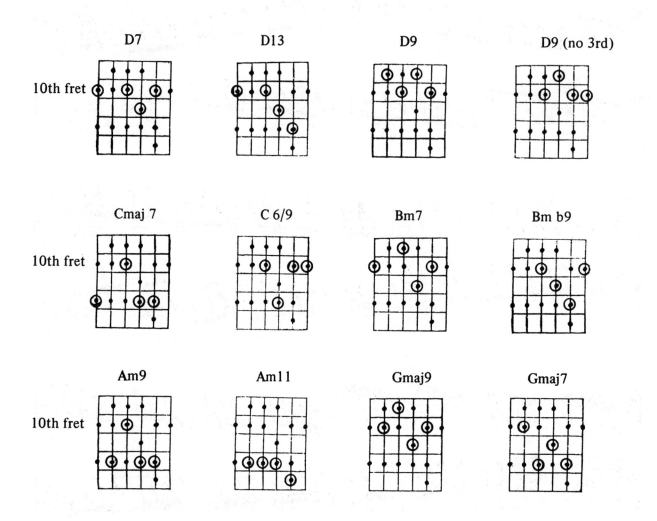

Here is an alternate fingering for "D" Mixolydian when playing over this popular "D9" voicing.

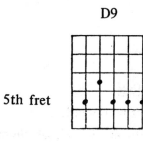

Here are some popular melodies based on the Mixolydian Mode.

Billie's Bounce   *By Charlie Parker*

The above example is a Mixolydian Mode usage in composition that also incorporates Nonharmonic Tones. These 'neighbor tones' such as the "B" Natural in the first measure are not part of the chordal accompaniment of the moment but create a feeling of anticipation by falling on the first beat of the measure and then resolving to the harmonic tone a half step higher. The same is true of the "G" sharp in the fourth measure. The "A" flat in the fifth measure suggests the "Bb" Mixolydian Mode.

It is possible to compose an entire twelve bar blues on just the Mixolydian Mode as long as we adjust the melody to fit the chord accompaniment. Here is a blues based on the "F" Mixolydian Mode.

Mixolydian Blues For Sarah   *By Mike Pachelli*

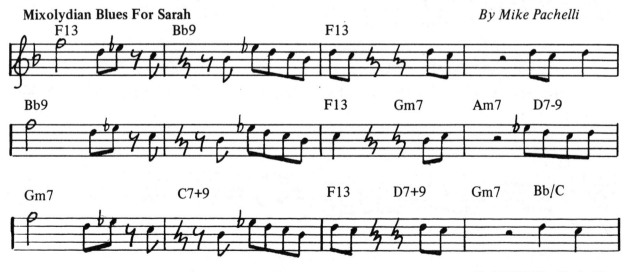

By thinking "D" Mixolydian as the parent scale against "G" Major type chords and ending our phrases to direct "D7" chord tones we create an unresolved effect.

"D" Mixolydian works well with "Am" chord types because of the II-V sound so popular in jazz improvisation.

When we use "D" Mixolydian against "Bm" type chords we emphasize the raised 5th, flat 9th sound as well as the minor 3rd.

"D" Mixolydian against "C" Major type chords really reinforces the "C" Lydian raised eleventh sound.

Reverse these examples and play "G" Ionian against "D7" type chords, or "A" Dorian, "B" Phrygian and "C" Lydian against "D7" type chords, etc.

The Blues Scale is a useful companion for the Mixolydian Mode. It is the basis of many "bluesy" sounding licks and can set, along with the Mixolydian Mode, a good foundation for improvisation on Blues changes.

Here is the "D" Blues Scale.

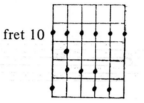

fret 10

The Blues Scale contains a Root, minor 3rd, a 4th, flatted 5th, 5th, and Dominant 7th.

Here are some phrases based on the Blues Scale.

Now combining the Blues Scale with the Mixolydian Mode.

AEOLIAN MODE

The Aeolian Mode is used widely in all types of music but probably most when improvising against one chord change in rock and fusion playing. It can be used against minor type chords or major chords for a "blues" effect. (Flatted third against major third) The Aeolian Mode is also used for a 'minor-raised five' sound that still sounds "within" the chord.

This is the "E" Aeolian Mode.

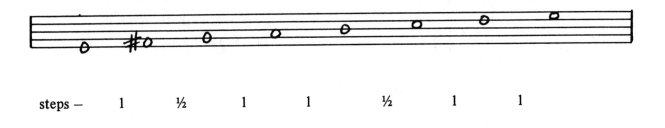

steps —   1   ½   1   1   ½   1   1

The Aeolian Mode has the same scaler series as the Natural Minor scale. It has a Spanish sound to it because of the half step between the 5th & 6th scale degrees.

example

The Aeolian Mode is a succession of whole steps except between the 2nd & 3rd scale degrees, and the 5th & 6th scale degrees which are half steps.

Chordal Characteristics . . . . .Minor third
Raised fifth
Minor seventh

solo usage — (against these chord types)

Em	Em7 +5	
Em7	Em 11	
Em9	(all 'E' Minor type chords)	

secondary usage. .all D7 type chords
third usage. . . . . .all C Major type chords
fourth usage . . . . .all B Minor type chords
fifth usage. . . . . .all A Minor type chords
sixth usage. . . . . .all G Major type chords

This is the Guitar fingering for two octaves.

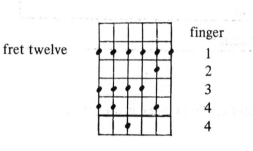

This position can be used when playing against "A" Minor type chords because it contains an excellent "A" Dorian fingering.

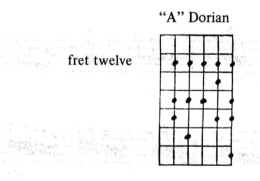

34

Here is the relationship between "G" Ionian, "A" Dorian, "B" Phrygian, "C" Lydian, "D" Mixolydian, and "E" Aeolian.

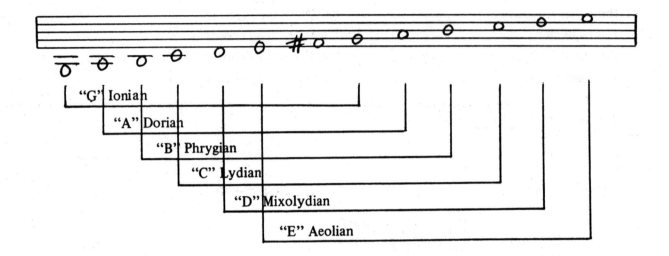

Suggested practice exercises for the Aeolian Mode. (To be done in all keys.)

PRACTICE SUGGESTIONS

Play the Aeolian Mode in all keys. Experiment with its' Spanish flair.

Be sure to use a metronome at various speeds.

Play "E" Aeolian against "D7", "C" Major, "B" Minor, "A" Minor, and "G" Major chord types.

CHORD RELATIONS

Em7	Em9 +5	Em 11	Em9 (add 11)

fret 12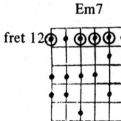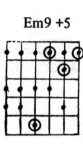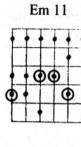

D7	D7	D9	Cmaj7

fret 12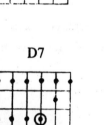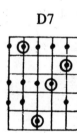

C6/9	Bm11	Bm7	Am7

fret 12

Am11	Gmaj9	G6

fret 12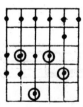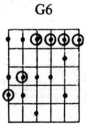

36

The Aeolian mode seems to be the most inherent sounding mode against a minor chord. This may be why it is also referred to as the "Natural Minor Scale." It works extremely well over minor ninth chords and like the Phrygian can be resolved to its' Tonic Major for a Spanish sounding effect.

(example)

By using an alternate fingering, the Aeolian Mode can be easily interplayed with the Dorian fingering by flattening the Dorian Modes' 6th scale degree. The two Modes have basically the same improvisational usage.

Dorian   Aeolian (alternate fingering)

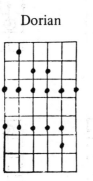   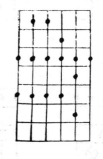

Here are some tunes based on the Aeolian Mode.

Blues For Kitty   *By Mike Pachelli*

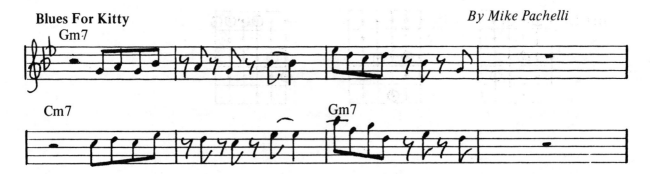

Eb9   D7+9   Gm7   D7+9

I Never Really Knew

By Mike Pachelli

Em9   Am7   Gmaj7   F#m7-5   B7+9

Cmaj7   B7+9   Cmaj9   Dm9   G13

By thinking "E" AEOLIAN against "G" Major type chords we reinforce the "6th" sound of "G" if we resolve to direct chord tones of "Em7" and this Modal correlation is very cohesive because "E" is the relative minor of "G" Major.

Gmaj7   (6th)

With "E" AEOLIAN against "A" Minor type chords we reinforce the "Am6" sound because of the inherent "F#". Also, by resolving to direct chord tones of "Em7" we can accentuate the "9th" and "11th" scale degrees of "Am".

Am7   (6th)   (11th)

"E" AEOLIAN against "B" Minor type chords strongly suggests the   + 5 — b9 sound, and by resolving the line to "E" the eleventh is firmly stated.

When "E" AEOLIAN is used over "C" Major chord types the flatted fifth or raised eleventh sound is predominant because the direct chord tones of "Em" do not alter the "C" Major sound since "E" is secondary minor to "C" Major.

"E" AEOLIAN against "D7" type chords reinforces the 'ninth' sound of "D7", and by resolving a line to direct chord tones of "Em7" we can put emphasis on the fourth and sixth scale degrees.

By thinking Polychordal and Polymodal we find new and interesting routes for improvisation. One needs only to determine the parent mode the particular phrase derives from, then to play the same phrase over alternate corresponding chords. This approach, although seemingiy systematic, can be a vital aid once filed in the memory banks.

LOCRIAN MODE

The Locrian Mode is the last of the seven diatonic modes. It is a minor mode with chord alterations flatted fifth, raised fifth, flatted ninth, and can be used for a raised ninth. For improvisational use it can create an "outside" effect against a minor chord change. The Locrian Mode allows for many interesting harmonic possibilities and is used much in jazz compositions and improvisations.

This is the "F♯" Locrian Mode

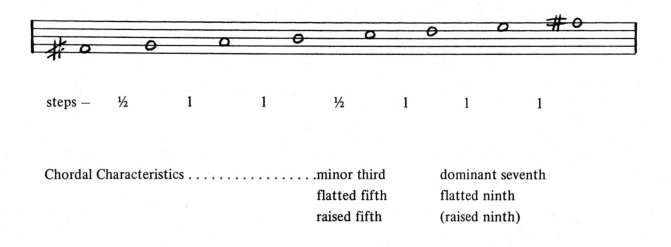

steps —   ½   1   1   ½   1   1   1

Chordal Characteristics . . . . .minor third   dominant seventh

flatted fifth   flatted ninth

raised fifth   (raised ninth)

The Locrian Mode is a succession of notes with half steps between the 1st & 2nd and 4th & 5th scale degrees and whole steps between the rest.

solo usage — (against these chord types)   F♯m   F♯m7   5

F♯m7   F♯m7 b9

F♯m7 b5   (all F♯m type chords)

secondary usage. . . . . .all E Minor type chords

third usage. . . . . .all D7 type chords

fourth usage . . . . .all C Major type chords

fifth usage. . . . . .all B Minor type chords

sixth usage. . . . . .all A Minor type chords

seventh usage. . . . . .all G Major type chords

40

Here is the relationship of all seven of the Diatonic Modes.

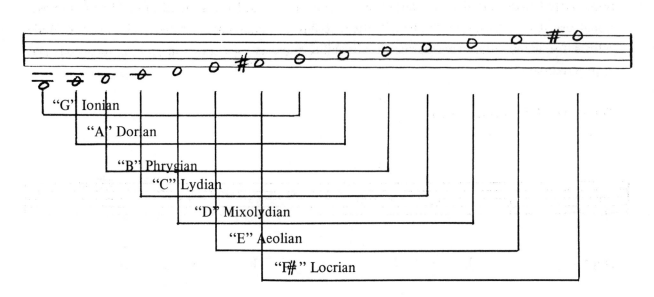

"G" Ionian

"A" Dorian

"B" Phrygian

"C" Lydian

"D" Mixolydian

"E" Aeolian

"F#" Locrian

The above 14 note "G" Ionian scale shows the total diatonic modal correlation.

Here is the Guitar Fingering for "F#" Locrian.

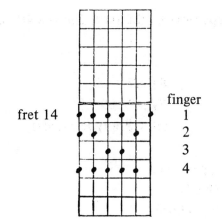

fret 14

finger
1
2
3
4

Of course this fingering
should also be used 8 ba
on fret 2.

These are the suggested exercises for the Locrian Mode.

etc.

etc.

PRACTICE SUGGESTIONS

Play the Locrian Mode in all keys. Listen to its' chord alterations.

Use the metronome at different speeds for the downbeat, then the upbeat.

Play the "F♯" Locrian against "Em", "D7", "C" Major, "B" Minor, "A" Minor, and "G" Major type chords.

CHORD RELATIONS

F#m7　　　　F#m7 b5　　　　F#m7 +5　　　　F#m7 b9

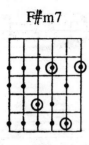　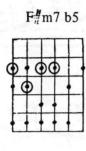　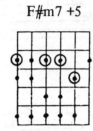　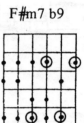

Em7　　　　Em7　　　　Em9　　　　Em11

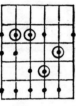　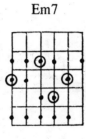　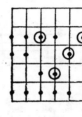

D　　　　D7　　　　D9　　　　D13

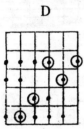　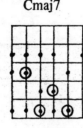

C　　　　Cmaj7　　　　Cmaj9　　　　C6/9 +11

Bm　　　　Bm7　　　　Bm7 +5　　　　Bm11

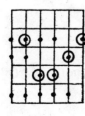　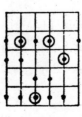

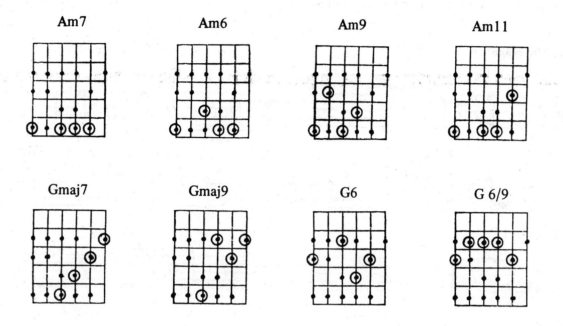

Am7   Am6   Am9   Am11

Gmaj7   Gmaj9   G6   G 6/9

All these chord relations can be made for every mode. That is, every modal fingering contains every relative chord fingering. The reader should take the time to find every chord relation in all the modes. You should be able to grab the chord you are playing against from any position you are soloing out of.

The Locrian Mode works well in some situations moving to the relative minor.

(Example)

44

Here are some tunes based on the Locrian Mode.

P.T. The Magician   *By Mike Pachelli*

Stop Over Anytime   *By Mike Pachelli*

Just the sound of the LOCRIAN Mode against a minor chord is mysteriously interesting.

For improvisational usage the LOCRIAN Mode can be thought of as starting the IONIAN Mode from a half step under its' tonic, since the fingering is identical on the guitar fretboard.

F# LOCRIAN

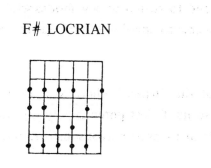

G IONIAN

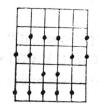

In this respect it is only necessary to think of the Major chord one half step above the Minor chord you want to play against, then use the IONIAN Mode and its' relative chord and modal substitutions for the desired LOCRIAN effect. (Example: for Am, think Bb IONIAN, C DORIAN etc.)

CONCLUSION

Now that you understand the total Modal correlation it should be easy to envision a clear picture of their importance in improvisation. Try to actually "see" the fingerings on the guitar neck to help you interchange positions of the same mode and to switch to new modes while playing off a particular chord or series of chords. Be sure to be able to 'grab' the chord out of every position of modal playing you are incorporating.

Remember to superimpose different modes against the "parent" chord you are soloing from. This is when **'MODAL MASTERY'** is being used to its' fullest potential. By injecting different moods against a common source we open our ears to many polychordal substitutions.

Use this book as a reference for it will take years to totally master this concept. Experiment with its' many polytonal possibilities.

Good Luck!